VIOLIN 1

Folk Strings

For Strings or String Quartet
Arranged and Edited by Joanne Martin

Cover Design: Candy Woolley
Illustrations: Rama Hughes

© 2002 Summy-Birchard Music
division of Summy-Birchard Inc.
All Rights Reserved Printed in U.S.A.

ISBN 1-58951-146-8

Summy-Birchard Inc.
exclusively distributed by
Warner Bros. Publications
15800 NW 48th Avenue
Miami, Florida 33014

Any duplication, adaptation or arrangement of the compositions contained in this collection requires the written consent of the Publisher.
No part of this book may be photocopied or reproduced in any way without permission. Unauthorized uses are an infringement of the U.S. Copyright Act and are punishable by law.

INTRODUCTION

Folk Strings is a collection of folk melodies from around the world arranged for strings. Some of these tunes were part of my childhood, and I have many happy memories of the hours spent singing them with my mother while she played the piano. Others are melodies I discovered more recently and are included because I enjoy playing them.

Unlike classical music, which normally has an "authentic" version, folk music often exists in many versions with differences in the melody or lyrics. Sometimes several countries lay claim to a melody because a group of people moved to a new country and took their music with them. Most folk songs were sung and played for many years before they were written down, and their original composer is usually unknown. This collection includes melodies in a variety of moods and with rhythmic patterns that are representative of their country of origin.

The arrangements in *Folk Strings* can be effective with players at a variety of levels. Less experienced players can play the melody line, learning it partly by ear and partly by reading. Some pieces in the collection are easier than others, and teachers can choose which are appropriate for their particular group. In order to provide maximum flexibility, the collection is available in a number of instrumentations, which are the same as those used in *Festive Strings* and *More Festive Strings*:

> ***Folk Strings for String Quartet or String Orchestra***
>
> ***Folk Strings for Violin Ensemble***
> ***Folk Strings for Viola Ensemble***
> ***Folk Strings for Cello Ensemble***
> > For two, three, or four violin, viola, or cello players in any combination of these instruments
>
> ***Folk Strings for Solo Violin***
> ***Folk Strings for Solo Viola***
> ***Folk Strings for Solo Cello***
> > For use with: *Folk Strings for String Quartet or String Orchestra*
> >   or   *Folk Strings for Violin, Viola, or Cello Ensemble*
> >   or   *Folk Strings Piano Accompaniments*
>
> ***Folk Strings Piano Accompaniments***
> > For use with: *Folk Strings for String Quartet or String Orchestra*
> >   or   *Folk Strings for Violin, Viola, or Cello Ensemble*
> >   or   *Folk Strings for Solo Violin, Viola, or Cello*

The arrangements are in keys chosen to be accessible and resonant. Shifting has been kept to a minimum, and where a shift is required, finger numbers indicate the first note in a new position. A fingering in parentheses means to remain in the same position.

In *Folk Strings for String Quartet or String Orchestra,* the melody is passed around so that all members of the ensemble can have the opportunity to play the tune. Score and parts are marked with "Melody" and "Harmony" to help players bring out the melody at the appropriate moment. These orchestra arrangements can be played by a string quartet since the instrumentation is complete without the bass part. Most of the time Violin 3 duplicates the Viola part; where the parts are different, the Violin 3 part appears in small notes in the score.

Both rehearsal letters and measure numbers are provided. In the orchestra arrangements, some of the pieces have rehearsal letters A1, A2, B1, and so on. These markings need explanation only if a group uses the String Quartet or Orchestra parts together with the Solo parts or with the Piano Accompaniment. The String Quartet or Orchestra parts have the repeats written out, with the melody in a different voice the second time. In these pieces, A1 in the orchestra part matches letter A for the first time in the solo part, A2 matches A for the second time, and so on.

During the preparation of this project, I have imposed on the good nature of numerous friends, colleagues, students, and family members. They gave their time generously to play the pieces, and their suggestions were invaluable in the revision process. In particular I thank Karen Barg Camacho, Mary Helen Law, Carolyn McCall, Judi Price-Rosen, Patricia Shand, Fiona Shand, Ellen Shertzer, Carole Shoaf, the "crusty academics," Karin Erhardt, who provided the cello fingerings, and Karla Philipp, who did the bass fingerings and in addition once again provided a wealth of helpful advice.

Especially I acknowledge my daughter Shauna for her continually cheerful encouragement and my husband Peter for being, as always, incredibly patient and caring, even when asked to play yet one more draft version or to proofread one more folder of parts. Their support gave me the energy to complete this project.

Folk Strings is dedicated to the memory of my niece Alison, whose brief years were so full of the joy of life.

Enjoy!

Joanne Martin

Contents

Introduction	2
Swing Low, Sweet Chariot	4
My Grandfather's Clock	5
Moo-Lee-Hua	6
Alouette	7
Marianina	8
Don't You Go	10
Farewell to Nova Scotia	12
Yankee Doodle	13
She's Like the Swallow	14
Valencianita	16
Teachers' Notes	18

MARIANINA

Violin 1

Italy
Arranged by JOANNE MARTIN

DON'T YOU GO

Philippines
Arranged by JOANNE MARTIN

* See Introduction for explanation of rehearsal letters

FAREWELL TO NOVA SCOTIA

Violin 1

Canada
Arranged by JOANNE MARTIN

YANKEE DOODLE

Violin 1

United States
Arranged by JOANNE MARTIN

SHE'S LIKE THE SWALLOW

She's Like the Swallow - 2

* See Introduction for explanation of rehearsal letters

Valencianita - 2

TEACHERS' NOTES

SWING LOW, SWEET CHARIOT - United States

>Swing low, sweet chariot,
>Comin' for to carry me home.
>Swing low, sweet chariot,
>Comin' for to carry me home!
>
>I looked over Jordan and what did I see,
>Comin' for to carry me home!
>A band of angels comin' after me,
>Comin' for to carry me home!

"Swing Low, Sweet Chariot" is one of the best-known spirituals from the southern United States. Spirituals were composed and sung by African-American slaves and almost always express religious ideas.

This arrangement should be played with warm tone and expressive vibrato. The tempo should be free, but the rubato must not slow down the tempo. The harmonies contain many blues chords, and notes such as major sevenths in chords should be brought out. Moving notes in the inner voices should also be brought out, especially in descending chromatic lines.

MY GRANDFATHER'S CLOCK - Henry Clay Work, United States

>My grandfather's clock
>Was too large for the shelf,
>So it stood ninety years on the floor;
>It was taller by half
>Than the old man himself,
>Though it weighed not a pennyweight more.
>It was bought on the morn
>Of the day that he was born,
>And was always his treasure and pride;
>But it stopped short
>Never to go again,
>When the old man died.
>Ninety years without slumbering,
>Tick, tock, tick, tock,
>His life seconds numbering,
>Tick, tock, tick, tock,
>It stopped short
>Never to go again,
>When the old man died.

"My Grandfather's Clock" was composed by Henry Clay Work (1832–1884), who also wrote "Marching Through Georgia."

Col legno ("with the wood") is normally played with the bow turned upside down so that only the wood hits the string. In this arrangement, turning the bow sideways so that the hair and the stick both touch the string will allow the pitch of the notes to be heard, as well as the ticking sound.

MOO-LEE-HUA - China

"Moo-lee-hua" means jasmine tree, and the lyrics describe the beauty of the tree in full bloom. An Englishman named Sir John Barrow reported that this song was very popular in China when he traveled there around 1800.

This arrangement contains many fourths and fifths, in imitation of traditional oriental music. The accompaniment parts should blend into a misty exotic background against which the melody can sing. The tempo should move enough that each two-bar phrase could be sung in one breath.

ALOUETTE - Canadian, originally French

>Alouette, gentille alouette, alouette, je te plumerai.
>Je te plumerai la tête, je te plumerai la tête,
>Et la tête, et la tête, alouette, alouette, O!
>
>Alouette, gentille alouette, alouette, je te plumerai.
>Je te plumerai le bec, je te plumerai le bec,
>Et le bec, et le bec, et la tête, et la tête, alouette, alouette, O!

> Alouette, gentille alouette, alouette, je te plumerai.
> Je te plumerai le nez, je te plumerai le nez,
> Et le nez, et le nez, et le bec, et le bec,
> Et la tête, et la tête, alouette, alouette, O!

"Alouette" is one of the best-known French-Canadian children's songs and is sung in many countries around the world. Like many French-Canadian songs, it originated several centuries ago in France. An alouette is a lark, and this nonsense song describes how the singer is going to pluck the lark's head, beak, nose, and so on.

This arrangement is light-hearted, in keeping with the lyrics. There are a number of canonic entries. The descending chromatics and unexpected harmonies may be surprising, as may the rhythm in bar 38, where the time values are doubled to provide a built-in *ritardando*.

MARIANINA - Italy

> Tante volte mi decesti
> T'amerà sino al la morte
> V'o divider la tua
> Nella gioia e nel dolar, nella gioia e nel dolar,
> Nella gioia e nel dolor.
> Ah! crudel, tu m'ingannasti, E donasti ad altro il cor,
> Ah! crudel, tu m'ingannasti, E donasti ad altro il cor.

"Marianina" is thought to be of Neapolitan origin. Its rather melodramatic lyrics bemoan a young man's unrequited love.

In this arrangement, it is important to keep the inner voices light so that the melody sings. The harmony parts should use a brushed staccato bow stroke throughout. The melody should use a brush stroke for the eighth notes in the first section (e.g., bars 9–23) and a more legato stroke in the second section (e.g., bars 24–43). At letter G, the fermata should be held the way a singer might, before returning to the regular tempo.

DON'T YOU GO - Philippines

> Don't you go, oh don't you go too far Zamboanga,
> Where you may forget your darling far away!
> Don't you go! Oh, don't you go, for if you leave me,
> Oh, how can I without you stay?
>
> Oh, weep not, my dear Paloma,
> Oh, weep not, for I'll return.
> Oh, weep not, my little darling,
> I shall remember and I shall yearn!

Zamboanga is a city in the Philippines, located in the province of the same name.

There are a variety of rhythmic patterns in this arrangement. The melody is primarily in eighth notes and includes ties and syncopations. The bass line is mostly quarter notes, with an accent on the last eighth note of every second bar. The inner voices have a different syncopated pattern in eighth notes. When players can learn to feel each of these patterns, putting them together should be easier.

FAREWELL TO NOVA SCOTIA - Canada

> The sun was setting in the west,
> The birds were singing on every tree,
> All nature seemed inclined for a rest,
> But still there was no rest for me.
>
> So farewell to Nova Scotia the sea-bound coast!
> Let your mountains dark and dreary be,
> For when I am far away on the briny ocean tossed
> Will you ever heave a sigh and a wish for me?
>
> I grieve to leave my native land,
> I grieve to leave my comrades all,
> And my parents whom I held so dear,
> And the bonny, bonny lass that I do adore.

Nova Scotia is a province on the east coast of Canada. The melody is thought to be based on a Scottish tune; these lyrics first appeared in the 1930s. In the remaining verses we learn that the singer is being called off to serve in the navy.

This arrangement should be played in a gentle style, keeping the tempo moving. It is important to allow the melody to sing out above the harmony parts, which imitate the roll of the waves.

YANKEE DOODLE - United States

> Yankee Doodle came to town,
> A-ridin' on a pony;
> He stuck a feather in his hat
> And called it macaroni.
>
> Yankee Doodle keep it up,
> Yankee Doodle Dandy;
> Mind the music and the steps
> And with the girls be handy.

"Yankee Doodle" is one of the best-known folk songs of the United States. It is thought that the song was originally written by the British to ridicule the Americans in the early 1750s but that it became so popular that the Americans themselves adopted it during the War of Independence (1775–83). The "macaroni" likely refers to a fancy Italian style of dressing.

This arrangement should be played quite simply; the countermelody can be played teasingly. Players can take extra time to switch from *pizzicato* to *arco* (at letter A and letter D) if necessary. At letter D, Violin 1 plays a pickup to the countermelody while all other parts begin on the downbeat.

SHE'S LIKE THE SWALLOW - Canada

> She's like the swallow that flies so high,
> She's like the river that never runs dry,
> She's like the sunshine on the lee shore,
> I love my love and love is no more.
>
> 'Twas in the garden this fair maid did go,
> A-picking the beautiful primrose;
> The more she plucked the more she pulled
> Until she got her apron full.
>
> It's out of these roses she made a bed,
> A stony pillow for her head.
> She laid her down, no word she spoke,
> Until this fair maid's heart was broke.

"She's Like the Swallow" comes from the province of Newfoundland on the east coast of Canada. Many Newfoundland folk tunes are rollicking sea songs, but in this song the plaintive lyrics and melody express the longing and regret of lost love.

In this arrangement the melody must always sing out over the harmony parts. The style should remain simple, and it is important to keep the tempo moving. The inner voices should be played *legato* and remain lighter than the melody at all times.

VALENCIANITA - Venezuela

> Una Valencianita, que del cielo bajo
> Con el pelo extendio y en la boca una flor
> En la flor una rosa, en la rosa un clavel
> Y en la mano una nina que se llama Isabel.
>
> Isabelita me llamo, hija soy de un labrador
> Aunque voy y voy al campo no le tengo miedo al sol.

The lyrics are a poetic description of a girl from Valencia whose name is Isabelle. Images of flowers, countryside, and sunshine are used to indicate her beauty. The city of Valencia is in northern Venezuela in an area where cotton and sugar cane are grown.

"Valencianita" incorporates many features of Latin-American music, particularly the rhythmic pattern that alternates between two and three beats to a bar. As with so many folk tunes, the written rhythm looks quite unfamiliar. It may be helpful if, before they see the music, players sing or play groups of six eighth notes, accenting in such a way as to alternate bars of two and three beats (**1** 2 **3** 4 5 6   **1** 2 3 **4** 5 6). What is on the printed page will make sense once the player hears the sound of the rhythm. Adding percussion such as maracas can add a characteristic touch.